Color /

Early in *Color All Maps New*, Jack Bedell ⌐_ ⌐_
that savory foundation for Louisiana cuisine: brown it witɦ⌐_ ₁
poem after poem, he serves up images, stories, moments of encounter, rituals
of love and loss, and the deft adventures of an observant mind in ways that
enliven without saying too much. There is often a beat of silence, a gift of
reticence just after a poem closes, and you look back to see how he got you
there. Spare, deft, resonant—these poems take you into local kinship rich
with lore, where dreams show a snake pit, floods lap the porch, turtles rise for
biscuits, and "spirits of our kin / linger in the marsh as blue heron."

—Kim Stafford, Oregon Poet Laureate and
author of *Wild Honey, Tough Salt*

These are exquisite poems about fatherhood and family life and the memory
that is required to bridge all that love. Jack Bedell has fed the muses plenty of
great Louisiana food and they have bestowed upon him great duende and
heart. These poems are perfect gems on the page, and they resonate with the
maturity of a man coming to terms with his rightful place in this life. Land-
scape and home are central to this collection allowing the poet to sing and be
a conduit to family lore and memory. *Color All Maps New* makes masterwork
out of language, and delicious roux out of the human touch.

—Virgil Suárez, author of *The Painted Bunting's Last Molt*

Jack Bedell's poems bring light and spirit to even the smallest things in nature
and culture. The opening of a car trunk, the fine details of cooking, garden-
ing, fishing, and even cutting the grass find wise and generous eyes here.
These are also poems powerfully and lovingly rooted in the South Louisiana
landscape; mosquito hawks, crabs, snakes, and everywhere water: swamp,
bayou, river, spillway, and Gulf. Bedell's brilliant use of metaphor, the dis-
arming and comforting rhythm of his poetic voice, and his masterful use of
the thing unsaid, all make his poems feel like sun-lit spaces in a dark time.
His poems will make you believe in poetry again.

—Sheryl St. Germain, author of *Fifty Miles*

MERCER UNIVERSITY PRESS

Endowed by

TOM WATSON BROWN
and
THE WATSON-BROWN FOUNDATION, INC.

Color All Maps New

[Poems]

JACK B. BEDELL

MERCER UNIVERSITY PRESS
Macon, Georgia
2021

MUP/ P617

25 24 23 22 21   5 4 3 2 1

Books published by Mercer University Press are printed on acid-free paper
that meets the requirements of the American National Standard for
Information Sciences—Permanence of Paper for Printed Library Materials.

Printed and bound in the United States.

This book is set in Adobe Garamond Pro.

Cover/jacket design by Burt&Burt.

Library of Congress Cataloging-in-Publication Data

Names: Bedell, Jack, 1966- author.
Title: Color all maps new : poems / Jack B. Bedell.
Description: Macon, Georgia : Mercer University Press, 2021. |
Identifiers: LCCN 2020050711 | ISBN 9780881467772 (paperback)
Subjects: LCGFT: Poetry.
Classification: LCC PS3552.E2877 C65 2021 | DDC 811/.54—dc23
LC record available at https://lccn.loc.gov/2020050711

Contents

Acknowledgments   vii

Just a Beginning   1

I.

Lines for a Country Song,   5
Bourré   6
New Growth Moon   7
Couplets, Interstitial   8
Communal   9
Gulf, Waves   10
Scales, Light   11
Bulleye   12
Mestayer   13
Silkies   14

II.

Lines for a 13-Year-Old Todd Marinovich   17
Proche   18
Course Correction   19
Snake Pit   20
Crux, Issue   21
Sassaquois   22
[My AM Dial Finds His Voice]   23
Ruddock   24
Catch, Memory   25
Dream, Distraction   26

III.

Lines for Lake DeCade   29
Fall, Light   30
When They Turned the Banks   31

Kate Mulvaney in Maurepas   33
Porch, Stew   34
Island Road   35
Isle de Jean Charles   36
Behind the Camp   38
Nuage   39
Exhumation   40

           IV.
Lines for Jonny Wilkinson   43
Beignets   44
How Many Times   45
The Gacy Murder House   46
[So He Picks This Spot Off I-55]   47
Last Island, 1856   48
Last Island, Return   49
Prayer Does Not Have To   50
Space, Release   51
All of Us, And None   52

           V.
End of the Line   57
Island Deer   58
The Secret   59
Jefferson Island 1980,   60
Like Bread for Supper   61
Summer, Botany Lesson   62
Dream, Lines   63
Breakfast, Continuum   64
My Daughter Says *Tell Me*   65
Dream, in Open Chord   66

About the Author   67

Acknowledgments

"Fall, Light" and "Mestayer," *Birmingham Poetry Review*; "Snake Pit," *Briar Cliff Review*; "The Secret," *Cease, Cows*; "Last Island, 1856," *Construction*; "Bulleye" and "Space, Release," *Country Roads*; "Beignets," "Bourré," and "Sassaquois," *Deep South Magazine*; "Island Deer," "Prayer Does Not Have To," and "Summer, Botany Lesson," *L'Ephemere Review*; "Gulf, Waves" and "Island Road," *The Fourth River*; "My Daughter Says *Tell Me*," *Grist*; "Proche," *Journal of Wild Culture*; "Lines for Lake DeCade," *Kissing Dynamite*; "End of the Line" and "Just a Beginning," *Kudzu House Quarterly*; "Catch, Memory" and "Last Island, Return," *Louisiana Cultural Vistas*; "Breakfast, Continuum," "Like Bread for Supper," and "New Growth Moon," *MockingHeart Review*; "Kate Mulvaney in Maurepas" and "[So He Picks This Spot Off I-55]," *Occulum*; "Crux, Issue," *Oxidant | Engine*; "All of Us, And None," *Peacock Journal*; "How Many Times," *The Penn Review*; "Dream, Distaction," "Exhumation," and "Nuage," *Rabid Oak*; "Course Correction," *Radar Poetry*; "Behind the Camp" and "Dream, Lines," *Rising Phoenix Review*; "Silkies," *River Styx*; "Ruddock" and "Scales, Light," *salt-front*; "Lines for a 13-Year-Old Todd Marinovich" and "Porch, Stew," *San Pedro River Review*; "Communal," *Shenandoah*; "Lines for Jonny Wilkinson," *Snapdragon*; "Isle de Jean Charles" and "When They Turned the Banks," *Speak the Magazine*; "Dream, In Open Chord," *Sooth Swarm Journal*; "Couplets, Interstitial," *Southern Quarterly*; "[My AM Dial Finds His Voice]," *Sugar House Review*; "The Gacy Murder House," *Terrain.org*; "Jefferson Island, 1980," *Twist in Time*; "Lines for a Country Song," *UCity Review*.

"Beignets," *The Donut Anthology* (Terrapin Books); "Isle de Jean Charles," *Southern Ecology: An Anthology of Literature and the Environment* (Yellow Flag Press).

Just a Beginning

What a slow breath let out on the porch
as the sun rises over pine trees—

my wife teaching our daughter
to brown roux without burning flour.

I.

Lines for a Country Song,
Best If Used Before

Belly up to a bar in the city,
        an old stranger gave me
the best advice I could ever get—

Son, when your mind goes
        to thinking about changing,
don't change. Quit.

And I can remember looking down
        into my glass of Bushmills
wishing I was anyplace else,

maybe even digging around
        in the fridge to make you
something for breakfast.

But I knew then, and there,
        once that milk turns
it never does turn back.

Bourré

Our old men
            wait on Saturday all week—
      through daily mail,
evening news, roast
            three ways, three nights,
      made-up chores—
just to deal cards
            and be dealt to.

Theirs is true art,
            the grouping of hand
      by number and by suit,

the bearing of time
until card meets table.

New Growth Moon

If I could, I'd leave lowland
and pine forests behind,
      move away from rivers
      that ache for my backyard,
merciless Old Testament rains.

Lord, how would it feel
at the base of a mountain range,
      calm lake in the distance,
      night breeze whispering
without the smell of storm?

Let me hole up on a porch,
wood creaking under me
      like a raft. The moon,
      aglow over settling fog,
could turn treetops into waves.

Couplets, Interstitial

I've got my father drinking a second cup of coffee
every morning he stays with us. The first cup

just gets him talking about news he watched
after we all went to bed the night before.

The second brings stories of men
I remember in flashes—Mr. Gonsalin

from across the street, Mr. Toot
from the bayou side, Old Savoie

who took a settlement from the company
but died after the third check—all gone.

Most times, I could finish these stories for him
like lyrics from some Frankie Lane song

we listened to on trips to the Smokies.
Sometimes, though, he offers a drum solo

or horn flourish I've never heard before,
like the time he asked my mother to marry him,

over the phone, half joking before he left
for the air corps, how she passed the phone

to my grandfather who explained, in turns,
the making of a bed, and the lying in it.

Communal

Yesterday afternoon, my wife taught me
      blueberry plants come with all the parts
they need to bear fruit, both male and female.

To get one full of berries, though, you need
      to plant it right next to some blueberries
from a different family. The only way they'll fill

with blossoms and fruit is to cross pollinate.
      Swarms of bees bring the goods from one plant
to the next, and the lot grow healthy and prosper.

Two plants, a small garden, and enough bees
      to outlast our dog's urge to snap them
out of the air as they fly from bloom to bloom.

Such a simple equation, this. So sensical
      that togetherness, time, and a little help
will fill our bowls to overflowing.

Gulf, Waves

Big moon, breeze—my daughter hurries
to finish her sentence in the sand

before waves climb up the shore
like dogs sniffing panéed meat.

She wants to spell out the names
of all the people she loves,

but the closer the water gets,
the more she knows

she'll have to edit her list
on the fly, leave some names

behind in the air to beat the tide,
its hunger boundless, and time.

Scales, Light

Sides of perch slap the pond's surface,
red, then gold as they catch the light.

My sons throw biscuits towards the ripples
the fish leave. Turtles crawl off logs

to join the feast, and catfish rise
from the mud to kiss air. My daughter

watches the reeds on the far bank part
then come back together. She has no fear

of the dark thing sliding towards the pond,
only for the fish, cold and out of sun.

Bulleye

There's nothing as still
        as the gold eyes of frogs
shining in a bulleye's light,

frozen   giving   waiting
        for the gig to pull them
from shallow water.

Their flat stare knows,
        past the reeds,
a sun in full glory.

Mestayer

—Frank Relle Gallery, Royal St., NOLA

The horizon releases just enough light
to wake the surface of the lake

and climb into the very top
of the one cypress tree in frame

so that its leaves and branches
look newborn against starry sky.

I know this photograph is of a real place,
a swamp not too far from home,

but its stinginess of light
raises the devil of metaphor

I can't chase away with knowledge
that its dark is just dark, its big sky

is only sky. I tell myself
this tree is alone on the water,

not loneliness; this light is fading
but is not loss. These leaves

are green because they are leaves.
No need to say more than that.

Silkies

My chickens' numbers are dwindling.
Each morning I go out to check the coop,
another one of them is missing.

After the first went gone, I shored up the wire
adding staples at each post. With the next,
I looped cast nets over the top of their pen
to protect them from above. Now,

I'm sinking tin around the whole works,
digging a trench all the way down
until I hit water. The birds follow me
in my circle, pecking ground and chatting
amongst themselves, gossipy and white.

Tonight, they'll sleep fine, all huddled
together, feathers floating in the breeze.
Mud will dry on the shovel where I hung it,
and I'll lie awake feeling foxes circle
the fortress I've built, their frustration
spread out across the ground like fog.

II.

Lines for a 13-Year-Old Todd Marinovich

"If you are good at something,
does it mean you're meant to do it?"
—Todd Marinovich

One afternoon during the monotony
of practice, put everything you are
into your play fake. Hunch over
the ball. Roll into the open space
the edge gives you. Absorb it, brother.
If you take enough of that field in, the sun
won't set on this grass. Watch the back tip
of the ball as it leaves your forefinger.
Listen to it hiss as it spins into the sky.
It doesn't matter where the ball comes down.
Hell, who cares if it comes down at all?
Hold that tight spiral in your heart
always. The rest of your life, shit will unravel.
School, career, even the eagle of your father's
memory will flutter and fall to ground.
That ball, though, let it fly. Rip it
and remember. What more
could any of us be meant to do?

Proche

The old people say spirits of our kin
        linger in the marsh as blue heron.
                They can move only in sunlight
        and must dry their wings to fly,
spreading them into the wind.

When enough days have passed
        through their feathers,
                they can pull themselves
into the air, bones
light and hollow with grace.

Sometimes they can circle near
        the places they once loved.
                If they find the eyes
of loved ones, though,
        their bodies turn to mist,

        swell into night sky
        like the first moon.

Course Correction

After the river showed up in the front yard
        everything in the house began to lean.

The water drew us to the front porch
        when it was low on its banks, pushed us

toward the back walls whenever it rose
        at night. The first full moon yanked us

toward the windowsill so fierce
        we had to spin the foot of our bed

around to face the lapping waves.
        Daylight helped keep things settled

enough for work to get done. Old growth
        timber still had to be planed for lumber,

upland traps collected for winter food.
        Even then, the river's flow conversed

in ways the woods never could,
        and the world would not untilt itself,

whether the moon waned new, or no.

Snake Pit

A hole opened in my dream last night,
          dug itself deep into the bedroom floor,

rimmed with a brick wall and covered
          with chicken wire edge to edge.

It exhaled the old air of stories
          my father told me when I was young,

of snake pits and men whose hands
          marbled around bite marks, whose fingers

withered in odd numbers from moving
          snakes in and out of the pit

whenever seasons changed. Sounds
          rolled over each other and pulsed

at the bottom of the well. Colors
          writhed, even in the dark of sleep.

My father's words echoed, deep
          drips into the well, and out

around my room. Strange in a dream
          for so much of him to swim in a hole

with so many snakes. Stranger still
          to lie there knowing my hands

would have to clear the pit come morning
          when the wind shifted north to south.

Crux, Issue

No sun, no shadows
     spilling off the cane stalks,

this late wind reminds you
     there is winter somewhere
          north of the horizon.

Inside, neighbors sing their best
     Andy Williams between highballs.

You build a fort in the front yard
     out of loose bricks
          large enough to house
               the baby Jesus, calculate
          how long it would take
   to rescue Him from the manger
in front the church, wonder

how much time would pass
     before anyone missed the child.

Sassaquois

He leaves his mark high up
on all the trees along the trail,

and with it a smell so thick
black bears spin around three times
before heading toward open space—

no shape on the horizon, only a knock
or yawp to rattle herons from their nests,

his swamp no place for discovery,
just mist and mud, enough water
for trot lines and quick passage home.

[My AM Dial Finds His Voice]

Every time I stay so late at the bar
      they wash me out with a hose,

my AM dial finds his voice, clear and urgent,
while all music fades to static. Preacher Smith says

                    the ILLUMINATI controls
our NEW WORLD ORDER with the two GEORGE BUSHes
and SELECT members of the SCOTTISH Rite,

                    and if we had sense to FACTOR it,
we would ALL see the numbers of every IMPORTANT date
in JuDEo-CHRIStian history add up to 144 with a
deNOMinNATor
of 7, the formula for which we relieved from the PHOnecians,

                    so we, BROTHERS and SISters,
must clear our minds of all interference CAST upon us
by the WORLD WIDE WEB and by the iLUmiNAti,

                    and by the NUMber 7, so that

                    we can HEAR the good news HE is
singing,
hear it and praise it before this HUMble PREACHer's hour of
POWer
ends, and we all return to REGular programming.

Every time, by the blood of the Lamb. EVery damn time.

Ruddock

Skiff launch and quiet water,
not much else to explain this place.

Tree lines haunt the horizon.
A highway overpass slices through
what's left of the growth.

Hiss of tires overhead,
locust squeal, and soft waves
leave plenty lull

lapping the water bank
over the tips of cypress stumps

to hear a car trunk opening,
      the clumsy splash a body makes.

Catch, Memory

The shark flops, chomps. Its back
gray, parenthetical against dock planks.

My sons scramble for the net,
way too small to hold this fish.

Their deck shoes squeak against wood.
Sunlight bounces off dark water;

drinks bead up on every piling.
Mosquito hawks hover

on what little breeze there is.
Afternoon scrambles right to the edge,

the pier barely fit to hold its weight.

Dream, Distraction

My father believed
snakes hunted in pairs.

Any snake lying in the open

kept a partner coiled
                in a nearby bush
or dangling overhead
                from a roof's edge.

The body has no defense
                against a snake dropped
down the back of a shirt.

Live your whole life before
                trying to pin a snake
against a wall, he said.

Snakes invented
                          distraction.

In dreams, though, I still focus
                too much on the snake
curled up in its tree.

It does not help me to know
                the fruit it offers

holds the reflection
                of real sin slicing towards me
in the grass.

III.

Lines for Lake DeCade

Down the warped dock,
　　　boards frayed and leaning
toward the surface of this lake,

water going brown, then to froth,
　　　sand flies　　　mosquito hawks　　　trawling motors
hum in the gray light

of tired days　　heavy nets.　　　Lord
　　　of fin and wing and prayer
hold me here　　as long as you can

before the water shifts,
　　　brings its salt in.

Fall, Light

Late-day sun goes purple
        just above the waterline, and,
on top of each wave, the sheen
        winks like loose jewels—

Just enough glow for treetops
        to define themselves along the horizon,
for water to turn the black of wasps' tails,
        all shine, all sting.

When They Turned the Banks

Time shifted in the basin.

A tapir's jawbone and molars
            from a mastodon
lay scattered in the soil,

loose at water's edge,
                open to the air
                        like diary pages.

Wind passing through the pines
carried the smell of rain.

                ***

We would have been
                small in this place
when it was high prairie,

our fires holding
                tigers in the shadows,

the meat of horned bison
or ground sloth feeding us
                through the long winter.

How different the music of our prayers.

                ***

Our coastline writes
           another story each day
it retreats into the reeds.

Its shadows hold
           the din of mosquitos,

our blood the dew of their feasts,
           the buildings we leave behind
porch-deep in brackish water

boneyards for them to sift through.

Kate Mulvaney in Maurepas

                             The forest is born
Of water and storm, with space to swallow her days.

She will learn to cure all fevers with oak moss
And pulp from cypress knots.

Night brings tide moon:
                  Conjure,
                       Locust song.

From the moment she walks the road out of town
Into these shadows, she learns to eat only cold things.

People will visit her as long as they feel pain.

She will coat their shriven brows
                With fish blood,
                      Juice of grasshoppers.

                         When the water off her dock
Turns brackish, she will bolt her doors.

        Her bed is thirst, wet with sweat.

Porch, Stew

No wind,   no sun.   Nothing
safer   than a shot from the porch.
The last remaining   grass
runs straight   from Island Road
to the front of the camp,   easy target.
Not many bullets left,

                              way fewer rabbits,

the store an hour's drive
          to the mainland. Breaths
in and out   slower,
until trigger   pop.
Brown water   pulls
          land into gulf.

Island Road

Water bit at the road's shoulder all morning
like a child pawing hard candy from a jar,

each wave lingering a little closer to the blacktop
until, by noon, there was only water, and gray sky

between what's left of the island and the line
of horizon that marks the way to town—

to school and store, and grass-dry land—
that sometimes catches the glisten of sun

when the water tilts low enough.

Isle de Jean Charles

The location of the new community has not been chosen. Chiefs of the two tribes present on the island—the Biloxi-Chitimacha-Choctaw and the United Houma Nation—have debated who would be allowed to live there beyond the islanders themselves, and whether some islanders could resettle elsewhere. One of the planners involved in the resettlement suggested a buffer area between the new community and its surrounding neighborhood to reduce tension. Chief Naquin wants a live buffalo on site.

—*New York Times* Piece on
Isle de Jean Charles Climate Refugees

Forget about the taut line, stretched
between forefinger and cast net.

Forget about the densities of family,
and of time, binding old ones
to babies just learning to walk.

Forget about the days spent
working together after countless storms,
salvaging the whole island's memories,
spreading them out to dry in the sun.

When the water finally takes
the last ten percent of this island,
think only of Island Road, how
the road once offered the one way
to school, or town, or places past the horizon.

Soon enough, there will be no way back
along this road. Anyone who drives
around the barricade on the mainland
will find waves at the end of blacktop,
gulls floating over the ghosts of rooftops,
wind where there once was song.

What more buffer could be built
between here and there than this loss?
What more to ease the tension of others?
A live buffalo, perhaps, but no one
could guarantee the animal would care
to go on living so far from its rolling plains,
or that it could stomach our mainland's sharp grass.

Behind the Camp

*

my uncle stacked crab traps   soot gray
wire twisted   into empty blocks

bait and rope strewn in the grass
blue flies and fish heads   ready for work

**

the men cleaned our morning catch
wiped their blood-oiled hands

on the tails of work shirts
as worn as dock's wood

***

cast nets   spread along the banks
waiting for the sun to drop
closer to the waterline   for gold
light   breeze   calm
to sweep them into air   hope

Nuage

All along our coast, reeds are laid down by wind—
one long cloud, gray to the horizon,

soft breeze and shallow surf, low land
my children will never see, each tide
a quiet goodbye. Pelicans refuse

to leave their nests, closer
together each season, their sand
washing out to gulf. Soon enough

storms will brew offshore, water
will color all maps new.

Exhumation

—Pass Manchac
after Mai der Vang's "Offering the Ox"

When the swamp releases them
  from its silt—
  mist off water,
  squalls of heron sound—

they float to the surface
  as bright lilies on the lake,
  swell, ardent with secrets,
  stories unwilling
to tell themselves.

    Fingers curled to palms,
legs stretched straight for diving,
    they know the shape
  of given space.
    Skin palls toward blue
the color of rain sound.

  In such a small lake
with its belly full of places to sleep,
    they need not rush
  their dreams of light.
    Waves spread out towards the bank.
  Silence in their loss
  rises from the water as psalm.

IV.

Lines for Jonny Wilkinson

> I don't know what it is, but my frustration is so intense I start
> shouting at the walls, screaming obscenities. But I punish
> myself for my mistakes too. When my left foot lets me down, I
> stamp down hard on it. At one stage, I am so livid that, before I
> know it, I am sinking my teeth into my hand, trying to bite
> right through the skin between my thumb and index finger.
> —*Jonny Wilkinson*

Is there something in the pain that gets you closer
to acceptance, closer to allowing yourself
missed goals or overthrown passes? Maybe
it's a balanced ledger of debt and recompense.

I often catch frissons over memories of my shortfalls,
times I could have done something to help my mother
set our Sunday table, or could have told someone
I cared about how perfectly the light framed their face,

or made even a single step toward someone else's
needs. Would settling those debts on the spot,
with real hurt, have saved these shivers later?
Would actually biting my own tongue, right then,

help me live with all the unspoken words, every
lost chance to put comfort in someone else's day?
No matter how much we do in this world, there is
always more could-have or should-have left to echo.

It never matters how much blood you draw biting down
on your hand, how many marks you leave stomping
on your kicking foot. The shadow of perfection is dark,
and taking the next kick is our only light.

Beignets

I want to show my daughter
how much her grandmother
loved making beignet dough.

Such simple work:
metal bowl, warm water,
yeast and sugar,

eggs, milk, and salt.
A quick whisk, and cups
of sifted flour.

My daughter's hands,
shaped so much like Mother's,
would be perfect for kneading,

for making smooth this dough
as sticky as any memory.

How Many Times

can you pull
a crab trap to the surface

by string tied off to the dock

before you stop expecting it
to come up full,

crawling with blue
claws, paddle legs,

more meal than any man
needs, more

weight than the trap's wire
can bear,

just more—

The Gacy Murder House,

—Antieau Gallery, Royal St., NOLA

Why is it so easy to admire this dollhouse
hidden in the corner of the gallery,
its rooms so tidy, well-lit, pinked

with flowers, ginghamed in patterns,
molding and frames as white
as white allows? Is it the respect

its artist had for the spaces
that make such places homey?
Its tasteful furnishings? The neatness

of design allowing us to overlook
skeletons lining the crawlspace
beneath its floorboards? Portraits

of killers, clown masks, saws, drills,
duct tape, bottles of rubbing alcohol
so conveniently idle with purpose.

[So He Picks This Spot Off I-55]

Traffic north of the spillway peters out
      and the moon offers no light at all,
so he picks this spot off I-55

to drop the bodies he collects
      in the French Quarter. The breeze
coming off the lake cools everything.

He can hear the water moving
      toward shore below the overpass,
can sense the tops of trees swaying

just below the clouds. This weight
      he drops over the safety rail
does not need make up, or jewelry,

or the silence the water offers below.
      For him, it is *drigaille*, just waste
to leave in the swamp, like an old freezer

empty and all out of use,
      eager to sink to the lake's floor,
hold the water's slow burn.

Last Island, 1856

They had no dreams to guide them
           through the screaming winds,
no sense of what the waves meant
           bounding onto shore
like baying hounds at the base of an oak,
           only Reverend McAllister
and a carousel on the levee
           to lash onto for the night.

How like the end of time
           that storm must have felt,
how unhinged the island
           spinning around them,
the ferry from Bayou Boeuf
           broken and run aground
just yards away, its captain
           fishing bodies out of the surf.

Last Island, Return

The roof from the main house
           reached shore first, shingles
lapped into the reeds. Bodies,

both breathing and not, washed in
           for hours afterwards. Wind
blew waves in bursts, long past dawn,

pushed the mess inland, almost
           all the way to solid ground.
When sun broke through the next afternoon,

it must have felt like hope on the shoulders
           of the living. Two weeks lost, though,
with only rain to drink, praying

for food, their small flock
           sweated its way through purgatory.
Shore birds mocked them, circling

overhead, just out of reach.
           Mosquitos, nearly large enough
to eat, bit through their dinner clothes.

Could any of them have imagined,
           getting dressed for their last meal on the island
before the storm pulled them into this hell,

how sweet the meat of live crabs would taste,
           how blinding white the deputies' shirts would be
marching towards them from the horizon?

Prayer Does Not Have To

whisper with reverence while clouds
        thicken to purple in the sky.

It can percolate, chortle and climb
        like Coltrane's horn in "A Love Supreme,"

probing in fits and squawks, clearing
        a path upwards, then knocking over

all stones, until there is no right
        of way, no safe passage, nothing

but tympani and bass drowning
        all hope in distance. I've been

in that room where it's clear
        the storm is on its way, where light

diminishes its chord until harmonies
        fall off each other, breathless.

Let the thunder have its say. Open a door
        to the sizzling wind. Trust

the score to give each note space,
        each need voice, until the whole room

vibrates in half tones, raises itself
        into the sky. This loud song

can find a stable key. This kind of noise
        can beg light down with a cymbal's roll.

Space, Release

I am teaching my son to throw into space.
He sees motion and color, releases the ball
toward what's no longer there, always
behind his target no matter how soon
he releases the throw. His feet pat grass
in rhythm, motion and delivery
all good. His eyes, though, won't drift
beyond now. Strange to know
how much the future presses on his heart,
fourteen years old and so looking forward
to drink or girls or driving, so ready
to haul off toward the open arms
the horizon extends just out of view.
And yet how miserable hard it is
to help him accept the notion of *early*.

All of Us, and None

My father sleeps in the downstairs study
when he stays with us on weekends.
He prays out loud to himself each night
before he goes to bed.

                                    The first time
my sons heard him, they pulled me
out of the shower naked and dripping
because they thought he'd finally lost
his mind. The more we listened, though,
the more we heard his tone had sense.

Sometimes the rhythm of his speech
grows quick, and his pitch rises like a child
running inside to say he's set a fire;

sometimes the words come low and in bursts,
as if, after a game, he's telling me
he's seen me miss an open man
to throw some useless deep ball
to nowhere.

                        My boys believe now
he's speaking to God, that his prayers
prepare him somehow to rest at the end
of our long days. I know that could be
true. Lord, I've said those prayers myself!

My daughter says she knows for sure
he's talking to my mother because she's there
in his bed some nights to join in.

I've heard my father's voice enough
without listening to his words

to know he'd never waste that much
breath on one person.

                                      Whatever he's saying,

it's meant for all of us, and none.

V.

End of the Line

—for Maurice Manning

The old men back home claim they can tell
what's on the end of their lines
by the tug it gives when their hooks snag—

Backwash from flounder; dash
and trick from speckled trout.

But what of the giant catfish
that lies still in the silt
and waits their lines out?

Island Deer

No grass on their island, the deer ate
              fish from shallow pools,
         gnawed gum from shore reeds.

My uncle told us
              it had been decades
         since they'd grazed.

In my dreams, these deer
              stood motionless
         just beyond our back fence

waiting for one of us
              to slide plates of roast
         and gravy under the wire.

Night passed without
              a single twitch—
         only moonlight, slow

breeze and wanting,
              until morning
         washed our grass clean.

What a slow swim
              to our land
         they would have had

against the gulf tide,
              their snouts just above the surface,
         persistent like the heads of turtles.

The Secret

—Antieau Gallery, Royal St., NOLA

Her fairy tale of blue sky and quiet bugs
        presses itself into the bark of a black tree—

grasshoppers and mosquito hawks,
        damsel flies and beetles live

this story stitch by stitch, closer
        to the skinny robins in this tree

than any world would allow.
        To keep it all a secret, she binds

her red dove's head with linen ribbon,
        soft and gentle as a mother's palm

saving her child's eyes from blood,
        or sex, or a life too good to lose.

It's one thing for the dove to remember
        what it's seen, another to fly off and share.

Jefferson Island, 1980

One puncture drained the whole lake
              into a salt dome.

Then the drilling platform,
              boats, and trucks parked nearby
                  along the bank.

All down the same hole.

The island was no longer
              an island without water
                  to set its borders.

Silt bottom dried slowly,
              stared at the sky like a blank face,

until one night after a rain
              the water came back.

Pine trees swayed in the breeze
              coming off Lake Peigneur. Shore birds
                  swam in patterns between stumps.

First morning light brought
              the gift of fog settling
                  above the tusks of mastodons,

reminders this place will be,
              whether or not we are.

Like Bread for Supper

What—when the wind begins to sing,
and the lake, not yet ready for land,
swells in its giant bowl, and the dog
curls itself up as close to the basket
of warm laundry as it can get
without climbing in—draws her

to spread flour on the counter,
spill risen dough onto the surface
from my mother's balsa plank,
and lean into the kneading
makes me think of feeding thousands
from two *croûtes de pain*.

Summer, Botany Lesson

No matter how many blossoms I point out
      exploding overhead on our neighborhood walk,

my daughter isn't buying it. She's in love
      with the sound of *bougainvillea*, thinks

the word's so pretty, there's no way
      it stands for something real. She believes

I made it up, strung long vowels
      and kissy, soft consonants on a strand

of rhythm to make her giggle. I wish
      I could tell a story that would win

her faith, but learn to let it lie. Some truths
      beg for a fight. Some would rather

echo on branches in crooked light
      while you just walk off holding hands.

Dream, Lines

In these dreams, my father stands
inside our front door frame,

storm screen swung open,
can of Falstaff sweating in his hand.

I am push-mowing the yard,
doing my best to keep my lines

straight, alternating dark
and light like a baseball field.

My work is slow, every dip
in the yard pulling the lines

off square, making fluid
what should be set hard.

The whole time, he watches
each pass, not a line showing

on his face. If he cares
whether my pattern holds tight,

I can't tell from his sips of beer.
His eyes follow me, though,

and I know the cold air
spilling out the open door

means something, even
if my lines slant.

Breakfast, Continuum

My mother had mornings to herself
     most days, kids off to school,
Dad out in the field, eight on,
     four off. Time to make coffee
in the Dripolator, brown sausage
     for gravy, bring milk and flour
up to a boil, low and slow. Drop
     biscuits, cast iron skillets.
No high fires, no cans. No need
     to talk, unless the phone rang.

     ***

Sundays, my daughter wakes me
     with her breakfast order. She polls
her brothers first, then delivers
     the menu to me, her voice the most
morning-ready in the house.
     These days, biscuits and gravy gets
the vote more times than not. Stirring
     and stories, flour and milk, spoonfuls
of dough baking quick as I can manage
     before my first cup of coffee brews.

My Daughter Says *Tell Me*

Something about PawPaw.
So I take her to the fridge,
            pull down the yellow box
of Arm & Hammer from the way-back
                part of the top shelf
and hand it to her.

I put my fingertip right
            in the center of the logo
and tap it gently.

*PawPaw's muscles looked
            just like that when I was
your age.*

                        She holds the box
up to the refrigerator's light,
            tilts it back
                        and forth before returning
it to me, knowing it's something

I have to put back in its place.

Dream, in Open Chord

Against the grain of what any day could hold,
        the backyard grows thick with cane
and hawks wait on power lines along the horizon.
        Just out of view, my sons chase each other
throwing oyster shells and laughing. My daughter
        draws pictures on the driveway in blue chalk.
The moccasin we killed last summer
        coils near her in the shade. Inside,
my wife rattles pots out of the cabinet
        for supper. She asks my mother something about
tomorrow. The sun drops and rises, drops
        and rises. The hawks tuck beaks underwing.
The snake crawls off unnoticed. And the question
        just hangs there in the sweet air.

Jack B. Bedell is Professor of English and Coordinator of Creative Writing at Southeastern Louisiana University where he also edits *Louisiana Literature* and directs the Louisiana Literature Press. Jack's work has appeared in *Southern Review, Birmingham Poetry Review, Pidgeonholes, The Shore, Cotton Xenomorph, Okay Donkey, EcoTheo, The Hopper, Terrain, saltfront,* and other journals. His previous collection is *No Brother, This Storm* (Mercer University Press, 2018). He served as Louisiana Poet Laureate, 2017-2019.